EARTH'S CONTINENTS

North America

by Mary Lindeen

North America is the third-largest **continent** in the world. It is between two oceans. The Pacific Ocean is to the west of North America. The Atlantic Ocean is to the east.

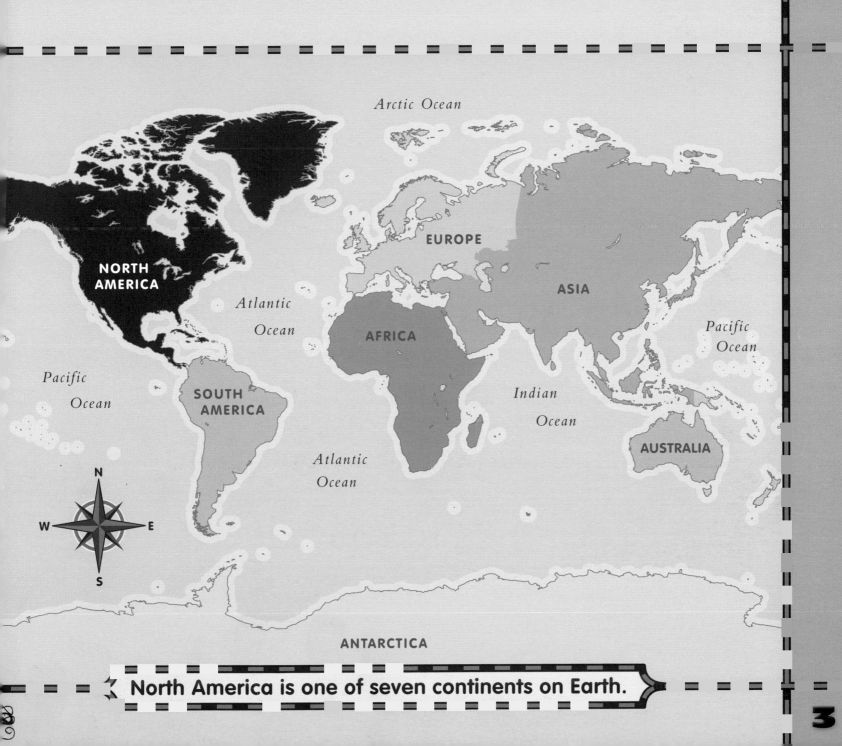

Arctic Ocean

EUROPE

ASIA

NORTH AMERICA

Atlantic Ocean

AFRICA

Pacific Ocean

Pacific Ocean

SOUTH AMERICA

Indian Ocean

AUSTRALIA

Atlantic Ocean

N
W E
S

ANTARCTICA

North America is one of seven continents on Earth.

There are four big **countries** in North America. They are Canada, Greenland, the United States, and Mexico.

Arctic Ocean

GREENLAND

CANADA

Pacific

Ocean

UNITED STATES

MEXICO

Atlantic

Ocean

Caribbean Sea

N

W   E

S

There are four big countries in North America.

The continent also includes some smaller countries south of Mexico. **Islands** in the Caribbean Sea are also part of North America.

This Caribbean beach is part of North America.

North America has high mountains and flat **grasslands**. It has **swamps**, forests, and deserts. It even has volcanoes!

Some North American forests have large redwood trees.

Some parts of North America are cold all the time. These places are in the north, near the **North Pole**.

Polar bears live in northern North America.

Other places are very warm all the time. There are deserts in some of these hot areas. There are **rain forests** in others.

This lizard lives in a North American desert.

There are big cities in North America. Many people live and work in these cities.

North America is home to New York City.

There are small towns and farms in North America, too. Farmers plant crops and raise animals.

Farms in North America help feed people around the world.

Many different kinds of people make their homes in North America. Most people speak English, Spanish, or French.

English and Spanish are two common North American languages.

There are many **famous** places to see in North America. Which one would you like to visit?

The Grand Canyon is a great place to visit.

Glossary

continent (KON-tuh-nent): A continent is one of seven large land areas on Earth. North America is a continent.

countries (KUHN-trees): Countries are areas of land with their own governments. North America includes many countries.

famous (FAY-muss): A famous thing is well known to many people. The Grand Canyon is a famous place in North America.

grasslands (GRASS-lands): Grasslands are large open areas of grass where animals can graze. North America has grasslands.

islands (EYE-lands): Islands are areas of land surrounded by water. North America contains many islands.

North Pole (NORTH POHL): The North Pole is most northern place on Earth. The coldest places in North America are near the North Pole.

rain forests (RAYN FOR-ists): Rain forests are hot forests where a lot of rain falls. Millions of kinds of animals and insects live in rain forests.

swamps (SWAMPS): Swamps are areas of wet, soggy ground. Alligators live in some swamps in North America.

To Find Out More

Books

Kalman, Bobbie, and Rebecca Sjonger. *Explore North America*. New York: Crabtree Publishing, 2009.

Sayre, April Pulley. *Welcome to North America*! Brookfield, CT: Millbrook Press, 2003.

Swinburne, Stephen R. *Coyote: North America's Dog*. Honesdale, PA: Boyds Mills Press, 2007.

Web Sites

Visit our Web site for links about North America: *childsworld.com/links*

Note to Parents, Teachers, and Librarians: We routinely verify our Web links to make sure they are safe and active sites. So encourage your readers to check them out!

Index

About the Author

Mary Lindeen is an elementary school teacher who turned her love of children and books into a career in publishing. She has written and edited many library books and literacy programs. She also enjoys traveling with her son, Benjamin, whenever and wherever she can.

On the cover: North America's Rocky Mountains stretch from the United States to Canada.

Published by The Child's World®
1980 Lookout Drive • Mankato, MN 56003-1705
800-599-READ • www.childsworld.com

ACKNOWLEDGMENTS
The Child's World®: Mary Berendes, Publishing Director
The Design Lab: Design, page, and map production
Red Line Editorial: Editorial direction

PHOTO CREDITS: Andrew Penner/iStockphoto, Cover; Alberto L.
Pomares G./iStockphoto, 7; Sherri Camp/123rf, 9; Big Stock Photo, 11,
21; Cody Wilkerson/Big Stock Photo, 13; Carlos Sanchez Pereyra/123rf,
15; Jim Mills/123rf, 17; Francesco Cura/Big Stock Photo, 19

Printed in the United States of America in Mankato, Minnesota.
September 2010
PA02076

LIBRARY OF CONGRESS CATALOGING-IN-PUBLICATION DATA
Lindeen, Mary.
  North America / by Mary Lindeen.
     p. cm. — (Earth's continents)
  Includes index.
  ISBN 978-1-60253-351-6 (library bound : alk. paper)
  1. North America—Juvenile literature. I. Title. II. Series.
  E38.5.L54 2010
  970—dc22   2009030013